Pankaj's Childhood

Pankaj Modak

Draft2Digital’s
Pankaj's Childhood

About The Author:-

My name is Pankaj Modak. I am a Short story writer. I was born in Chandaha, a village in India, which is located in the state of Jharkhand. My father is

Shankar Modak and my mother is Lalita Devi. I have two elder brothers and an elder sister.

Contact e-mail address:- pankajspersonal23@gmail.com

I was born as the sixth son after my father's first two children died due to illness. When I was a kid, when I used to go to the Anganwadi to study, many times my elder brother and friends would run away before the school was over and I would be left alone there. In the year 2011, I was enrolled in the government school located in our Chandaha village. After one year, I went to the second class. The door of that class was torn. So, during lunch time, I would go inside the class with my friends through that torn door and take out my books and run away. We would reach home via the fields. For doing this, sometimes I would get scolded at home and sometimes beaten by the teacher in the school. Many times, while playing with the children of the houses near our house, I would get into fights. Many times, I would get scolded by my father and mother over food items by lying. Even then, my mother would forgive me. Whenever my family members or teachers would ask me - what will you become when you grow up? I said:- Scientist. It was evening time. A tractor was parked near the Ganesh temple. We used to play there with the children of the village in the evening. I was riding on the tractor's wheels in the evening. While playing, my hand slipped and I fell down from the tractor. I lay unconscious on the ground for a few minutes. After that, a person from the village brought me to my house on his shoulders.

I recovered after a few days. It was the year 2013. That year I was around eight years old. It was morning time. Me and my middle elder brother and one or two children from our village, we set out to take a bath at a dam called Saag. We reached the dam. At that time the dam was full of water. A few months ago when the dam had dried up, a person from the village had dug a well in the middle of the dam. Which was quite deep. People used to fill water from it. But when it rained after a few more months, the dam was completely filled. The well remained there. We entered the water. I did not know how to swim at that time. They started swimming. I started playing with the water. They went to the bank and started applying soap on their bodies. I kept playing with the water. I started going towards the water. I reached quite deep.

One of my feet was on the ground and the other was above the well. My head came under the water. I was pointing my hand upwards. After about ten or twelve seconds, a village girl saw my hand. She was like my elder sister. Without any delay, she swam quickly to me and caught hold of me and brought me to the bank. After that she brought me to my home. My parents and family members came out. My life was saved. After a few months. Once, I was gripped by a long fever. I took medicines of many doctors. But the fever was not getting cured. After that, father took me to a big doctor in the city. There was a lot of crowd there. So it took a lot of time. Therefore, a big screen TV was installed there for the entertainment of the people. A comedy movie named Awara Pagal Deewana was playing on it. Our turn came. Father told everything. The doctor examined us for some time and wrote something on the slip. I thought that he must have prescribed some medicine. But later I came to know that I had to be given an injection. In the morning, out of fear of the injection, I would run away from home.

Then father would catch me and bring me. In this way, after getting ten injections in five days, the fever was cured. It was the year 2015. It was summer season. At that time my age was around nine years. Many times, when father went somewhere, I or my middle elder brother used to stay in the shop. It was morning time. I and my friend started walking towards the government school together. At that time I was studying in the fifth class. After some time we reached the school. After the prayer, we sat on the benches. The class teacher came. He started teaching in the class and we started studying. After some time, Sir had to go to another class due to some work. My friend and I sat on the bench and started playing. While playing, my friend punched me on the nose. At that time, I was a quarrelsome person. I used to fight with anyone. At that time, anger was always on my mind. After getting punched, I thought that I will also punch him on the nose. I also punched him on the nose. There was already a wound on his nose. That is why blood started flowing from his nose. All the children in the class were watching us. I got very scared. I could not understand anything. What should I do? What will happen now? Many children started giving advice. Take him home. On the other side, a child brought the teacher to the class. Blood was continuously flowing from his nose. The teacher was shocked to see this and started hitting me on my back with a stick. I kept saying while crying. Sir, he already had a wound on his nose. The teacher there was also shocked to see the blood. His white shirt was completely wet with blood. My friend was lying on the first bench of the class.

After the beating was over, the teacher said- Leave the school. I took my notebook and the book given by the school and left it there and started walking towards my home. At that time, I was like a child, so I said to myself- I will never go to this school again. I reached home and started watching TV. Even now I was scared. After a few minutes, his parents came to our house and started scolding me. I became more sad. After a few days, my elder sister got married. About a month after that incident, he became completely healthy. After a few days, I and my friends started going to the same school again. After this incident, I started concentrating more on studies. The year was 2016. Elder sister On the insistence of my younger brother, my father bought me a 3G smartphone. After my elder brother, both of us brothers used that smartphone. Many times I would snatch the smartphone from my middle brother and start playing games. He would keep watching. He would feel very bad. But he would not say anything. I was not that smart at that time. I used to go to school wearing half-pants and an old white shirt. At that time only tribal castes and girls were given uniforms. It was the day of the examination. I was standing outside a shop situated at a little distance from the school. A mischievous boy came from behind and started running after putting ink on the examination slate. I also started running after him. My elder brother was going to tuition on a bicycle. He caught hold of that boy. That boy apologized and went away from there. In the sixth class, the students were made to sit outside in the cold. A boy sitting behind was hitting me on the head with a toffee. Due to some work, the teacher had left from there for some time. As he was disturbing me for a long time, I stood up and pushed that boy. Other students were laughing at that boy. The next day, that boy came to school with his younger brother. They would hit me with their hands and run away. This happened many times and I started crying. After that, they stopped doing this. It was the year 2017. At that time uniforms were distributed again and all the students got them. I wanted to get full-pants, but because I was short, I got half-pants. After a few weeks. Two people from the steel company organized a running competition and a writing competition. Students were making fun of me. Because at that time I was a fat boy. Still I participated in the running competition and writing competition. I and my friend, most of the times used to sit on the last bench of the class. But this time other students pushed us ahead. We started writing essays on Mahatma Gandhi ji. Both of us wrote ten lines and sat in such a way that we would get the mono prize. The running competition took place. But I probably remained at fifth position. When the result was declared, we came to know that we have failed and we are not going to get anything. With sad faces, we returned home. A few months later, I was studying in 7th standard. A person from a private school came to our class which was located near Bijulia turn. He told me that a quiz competition is going to be held and started giving information about it. After that I started studying for many nights. The day of the competition came. We sat on the bike and started going to the competition building.

But later we came to know that the day of the competition has been changed and it is going to be held in the next week. The competition started in the second week and we reached there. I started filling the answers of the questions thoughtfully. In the evening, we returned home. It was the last month of the year. The year 2018 came. I came to 8th standard. In my free time, I started reading the chapters of biology present in the science book. I started getting interested in reading the chapters of biology. I started feeling that I will become the next biologist. After a few weeks, that person came and started calling out the names of the winners in the competition. I was sitting on the last bench of the class with hope. He said that Pankaj Modak has secured the second rank. My happiness was clearly visible on my face.

Other students were clapping. I was given a silver medal and my photo was taken. Earlier, a Kabaddi competition was organized by a tuition. I had lost in that too. This was the first time I had received a prize. I returned home happily. My parents were also very happy. At that time, I was around twelve years old. A few days later. It was winter season. One day, I woke up in the morning. After waking up, I thought of using my mobile for a while. That mobile belonged to my elder brother. Which worked on 3G network. Since it was a cold day, the scene outside was like night. I picked up the mobile and, covering myself with the mattress, watched a pornographic video of a web series on the online player. After that, I started searching for similar videos. After a few days, I started watching pornographic videos from the web browser. I used to watch those videos alone or at night. Gradually, I became addicted to those videos. I was moving towards mental illness. A few weeks passed. Now I had started to feel sad. I did not feel like doing anything. Whenever I saw a girl, woman or an old woman, I would start thinking obscene things about her. When I prayed in school, I would stand there for some time even after the prayer was over. Then my friend would shake me from behind and I would come to my senses. Sometimes I would sit silently in the house. The family members would think that I was suffering from the evil eye of people. That is why they would get me exorcised by many tantriks. But there was no effect. The family members would ask me what happened? What is happening? But I could not say anything. One day my elder brother got angry and scolded me, so I started crying. One day my father took me to a hospital in Bokaro. Where the doctor used to treat diseases related to the head. The doctor was to come in the evening. We sat for a long time. We had come in a rented car. Only two cars used to go to our village. One train had already left. The second train was yet to leave. After some time, father came to know that the train was about to leave. Due to the fear of missing the train, we came back home without consulting the doctor. At that time, I was fat.

So everyone thought that this could be the reason for obesity. So now father told me that I am not getting any treatment. He started taking me for a run every morning. A few days ago, I had stopped watching porn videos. I started watching good videos and movies on TV and mobile. I started running in the morning, getting fresh air and going out in the midst of nature. I started growing trees and plants. Slowly, I started recovering from this disease. It took me several months to recover from this mental illness. After these incidents, many changes came in me. I reduced fighting, stopped snatching my mobile, and started being sad and quiet. In the year 2019, I gave my board exams for class 8. After that, I went with my friends to the City Park in Bokaro city (where there were beautiful and large number of trees and flowers. White lotus flowers were blooming in the pond and the old bridge was situated there. The beauty of the place was captivating) and City Mall. The result of class 8 came and I came to know that I had got B-grade. I was a little happy and a little sad. My eighth grade teacher and tuition teacher had high hopes that I would get first. But their hopes remained just hopes. After that. Father got me admitted in a private school located in Sialjori village. While studying in that school, I fell in love with a girl student and this love remained limited to that. In the year 2020. A quiz competition was started in a private school in Talgadia by a book company. I reached there in the afternoon with my father. After that father left from there. After the competition was over, the result was declared. I came to know that I had failed and could not make it to the top-10. It was about to be evening. I took my bicycle and started going with them. After going some distance, they stopped there. I was in the front. Someone had fallen from the bike there. That's why they were waiting there. I thought it would be night. So I left from there alone. After reaching some distance, there were two paths ahead. I did not remember which route would take me home. So I slowed down my cycle. Just then a girl came from behind. She was from our village. I came to know which route was right. I also started walking on that route and reached my home. That very year, I left the blazer pant of the uniform and got another black pant stitched. Which was loose. Later, because of that pant, I was going to get the tag of an obscene boy in school. When I would wear that black pant and sit on the bicycle or on the bench in the class, the pant would look swollen in such a way as if the penis had become excited. All the students would start laughing. I started getting worried about how to fix the pants. So most of the times I used to go to tuition wearing white pants. In the month of February 2021, a quiz competition was to be organized by the steel company. The selection process started. In which four students were being selected from each tuition batch. I thought and thought and gave the quiz competition test. In which I got selected.

But I failed in the race competition test. But I was happy that I got selected in the quiz competition. My friend had not given the test. That is why he was not selected. It was the month of February. That night I kept reading and writing objective questions and answers for the quiz competition till late night. I filled many pages of the copy by writing. We reached the school at around 9 in the morning. The tuition teacher was present there. Students of Chandaha and Sialjori batch were present here. Who studied in that school. After about one and a half hours, the company bus reached there. We sat in that bus and started moving towards the competition building. The green view outside the windows of the bus looked pleasant. After some time, we reached there. The land there was very clean and good houses were built. After the examination, we went inside. The competition building was very big and luxurious. The decorations were done very well. Students of different batches were seated. There were two girls and two boys in our batch. Boys and girls were seated in separate lines. I sat in the last row. I was a little nervous. Before the competition started, a motivational speaker inspired all the students with his thoughts. The competition started. In the first round, four options were given along with the question. The answer had to be given in just 60 seconds. 10 marks were awarded for the correct answer and 5 marks were deducted for the wrong answer. Our score in the first round was quite low. But we had scored enough to play the last round. Many batches were eliminated in the first round itself. Some batches were selected in the final round. Only a few of our teams were in the last rank. But we had made it to the final round. Lunch time started. It was afternoon. All the students boarded the buses and went towards the canteen. They ate and drank there and came back. After some time, the final round started. But in the final round, pictures were shown on the screen through the projector and questions were being asked. Whoever knew the answer, pressed the buzzer alarm and answered. The series of questions and answers started. The scores kept fluctuating. Tetoliyan batch secured rank-1, Chandaha batch secured rank-2, Excel-30 batch secured rank-3. But the Sialjori batch which was performing well since the first round, went to the last rank with 0 score. There was no limit to the happiness on our faces. Happiness was visible on our faces. After some time, prizes were distributed and photos of the winners were taken. After that, the students sat in their respective buses and started going towards home. It was evening time. Our cycles were kept in the school. So we reached the school first by bus and then started towards home by cycle. After a few weeks, the tenth class examination started. But due to the Covid-19 virus, the examination was cancelled and the students were promoted on the basis of the ninth board result. That year, we left the school and got enrolled in the eleventh class. Also, said goodbye to that black pant forever. From tenth to eleventh class, I had solved so many maths problems and my interest in maths had increased a lot. It seemed that I would become the next mathematician. Father got me enrolled in a college located in Bandhdih. An old friend had taken arts. So, along with a new friend, I started going to tuitions about four kilometers away by cycle. I used to go to the examination building with my elder brother or father. My elder brother and the boys in the neighbourhood would say - hey, you have taken science and are taking tuitions only for maths. You will fail. But I was confident. I started studying all the subjects of class 11th every day, except Sundays. The year was 2022. The results of class 11th board exam were good and I secured first division with more than 60% marks. My parents' faith in me regarding studies got stronger. After that, I went to class 12th. But my interest in maths and other subjects started decreasing. I started getting interested in reading and writing stories. I started writing stories every week. I started reading story books, like

Manasarovar's books. I started going for tuitions only occasionally. After insisting for a long time, in the month of June, father bought me a 4G smartphone. I was very happy to get my own smartphone for the first time. The morning of October 2022. I come to know that my elder sister's husband has committed suicide. The whole family was drowned in grief. Sounds of crying and wailing could be heard. A few months later. The year was 2023. My elder sister returned to her maternal home with two small children. Due to lack of interest, I was not able to study the subjects of 12th class properly. Finally, I failed in the 12th board examination. After a few weeks, on the insistence of my elder nephew, my father bought a baby pigeon for him. My nephew was busy playing and misbehaving. Due to which he did not pay attention to that pigeon.

My nephew's mother used to feed and give water to that pigeon daily. Some days passed. One day, looking at that pigeon, I thought why not make it fly. Now I made that pigeon fly once every day. But during the flights, it would collide with a wall while flying. So now I took it out of the house and made it fly. Days went on passing like this. That pigeon had a type of disease. Due to which blood started coming out of its eyes and yellow spots used to form on its eyes. Due to which it could not see anything. Family members would tell me not to make it fly, not to touch it. But I did not listen to them. But when I saw that it was unable to see, I stopped flying it. But I started flying it once a day. It was winter season. It was around ten or eleven o'clock on the clock. I flew it for some time and put it in the sunlight on the ground. There was a smile on its face. I felt good seeing it. The next day. It was morning time. I heard that the pigeon died. I could not believe it. So I went there to check and see. I saw that the pigeon was lying lifeless on the ground. Due to cold its whole body had become stiff. I shook it a little. But it had already slept in the lap of death. I thought to myself. If only this baby pigeon had not been separated from its mother, then today it would have been flying with its mother somewhere in the blue sky.

www.ingramcontent.com/pod-product-compliance
Lightning Source LLC
La Vergne TN
LVHW010118170826
845678LV00012B/2484